A Four-Week Study for Adults

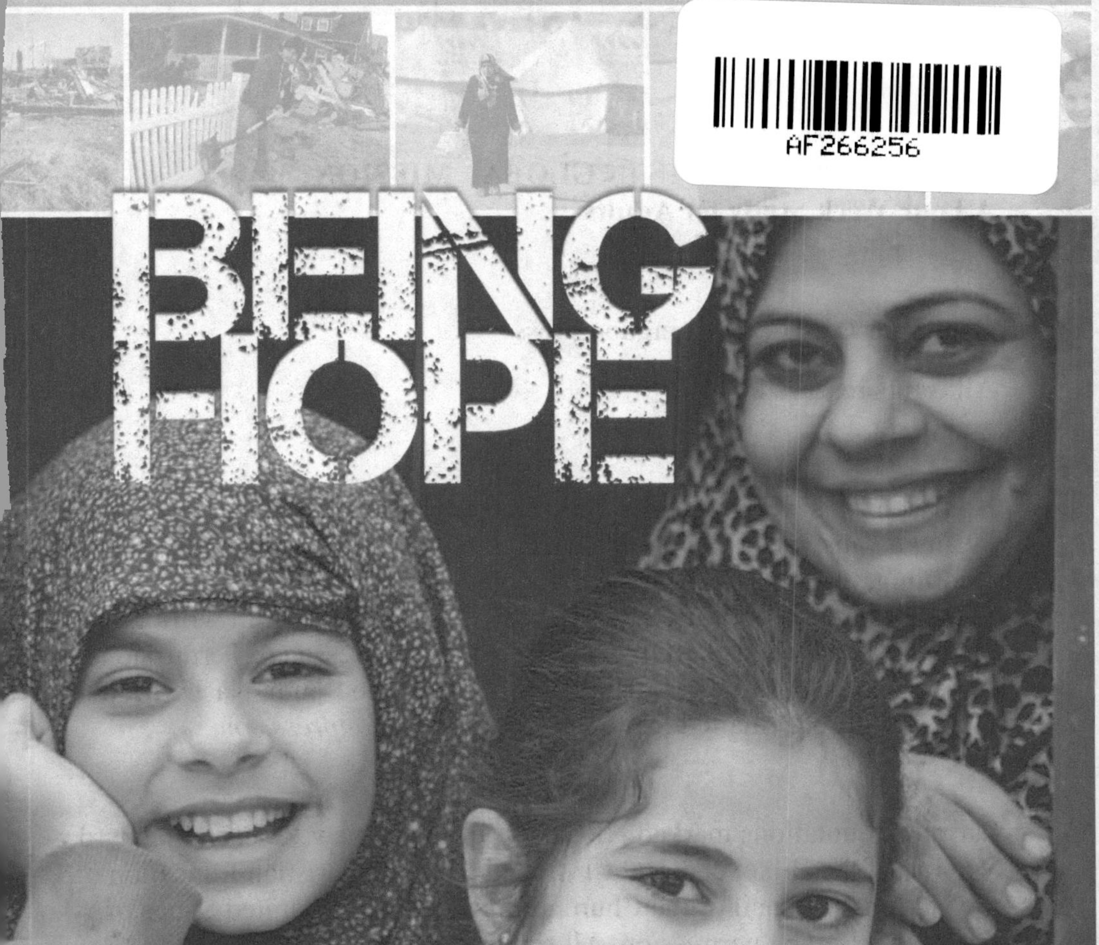

BEING HOPE

United Methodists in Global Mission

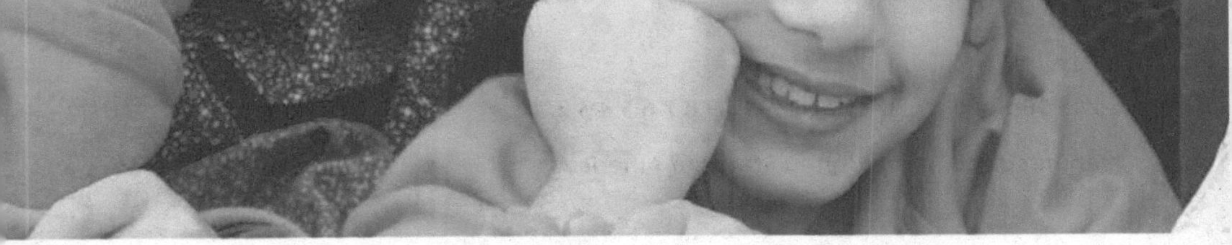

Larry Beman

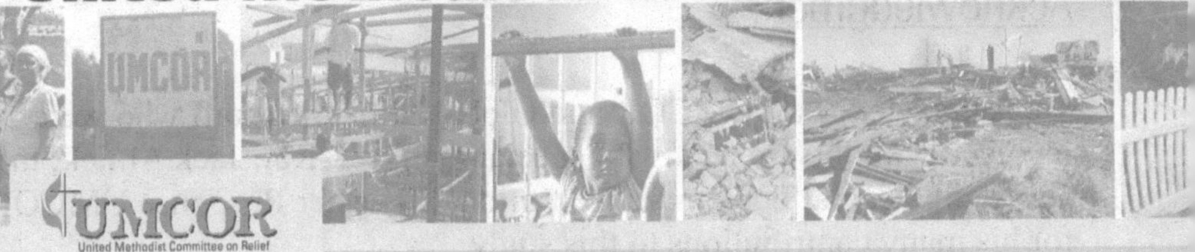

BEING HOPE
UNITED METHODISTS IN GLOBAL MISSION
A Four-Week Study for Adults

14 15 16 17 18 19 20 21 22 23—10 9 8 7 6 5 4 3 2 1

Manufactured in the United States of America

Acknowledgments

We acknowledge all UMCOR and Global Ministries staff who were involved with this project, with special thanks to Rev. Jack Amick, the Assistant General Secretary, International Disaster Response UMCOR, for his many contributions to this study.

Vision

As the humanitarian relief and development arm of The United Methodist Church, UMCOR transforms and strengthens people and communities.

Mission

Compelled by Christ to be a voice of conscience on behalf of the people called Methodist, UMCOR works globally to alleviate human suffering and advance hope and healing.

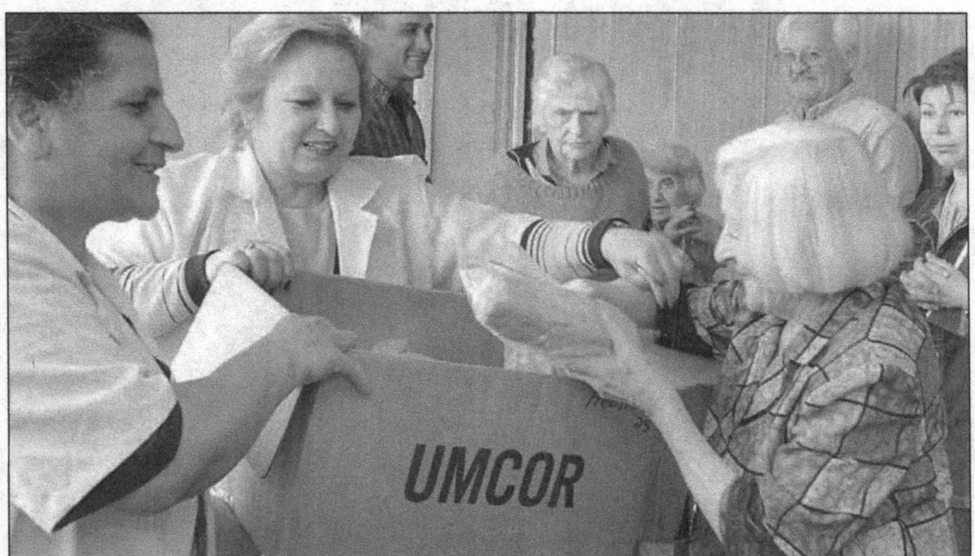

Churchwide Mission

To lead your whole church in the *Being Hope* study, look for these related resources:

Being Hope Four-Week Study for Youth (ISBN: 9781426782589)
Being Hope Four-Week Study for Children (ISBN: 9781426782626)
Downloadable Social Media Kit, available at *http://www.abingdonpress.com/BeingHope*

Contents

Rejoice in hope,
be patient in suffering,
persevere in prayer.

Romans 12:12 (NRSV)

Introduction

Once upon a time not so long ago, an aid worker was assisting a homeowner who suffered terribly as a result of a devastating hurricane. Their conversation wound its way toward the church and its response to this tragedy. The homeowner noticed the Red Cross facilities, the FEMA trailers, and other governmental agencies. Then the homeowner complained, "Where is my church when I need it most?"

The aid worker asked:

"Do you see that semi-trailer truck over there?

"Yes."

"Do you see the markings on the side of the trailer?"

"Yes."

"What do you see?"

"A cross, with a flame beside it."

"That truck was sent here by the United Methodist Committee on Relief. Your church has been here all along."

It is not much of a stretch to say that the United Methodist Committee on Relief (UMCOR) is there whenever and wherever there is disaster around the world. Often working with partner agencies, UMCOR lives its goal "to assist the most vulnerable persons affected by crisis or chronic need."

Although UMCOR has been around since 1940, and many United Methodists have an understanding of UMCOR that dates back to their childhood, there is always more to learn about UMCOR. Here are a few facts about UMCOR that sometimes surprise United Methodists.

UMCOR reaches out to people in need in over eighty countries.

In 2013, UMCOR responded to over 30 disasters in the U.S. and other countries, provided more than 302 grants to partners in over 56 countries, and provided response, development, and global health grants in excess of 13 million dollars.

The One Great Hour of Sharing offering, collected by United Methodist churches, pays for UMCOR's administrative support, so **100 percent** of any designated giving goes to the specified project or work area.

UMCOR began in 1940 as the Methodist Committee for Overseas Relief. In 1972, it expanded its mission to include projects in the United States.

In the aftermath of Superstorm Sandy, nearly one thousand UMCOR volunteers helped with recovery efforts.

In most situations outside the U.S., UMCOR does not deploy volunteers to respond to disasters, but works primarily with specialized international non-governmental organizations (NGOs) and, where appropriate, local Methodist entities and the local population.

UMCOR not only responds to disaster, but also engages in long-term development projects where possible.

UMCOR does not work in a vacuum. Its work is thoroughly grounded in both Scripture and the Wesleyan tradition. From beginning to end, the Bible consistently demonstrates that God has a passion for those most in need. From the law codes of the Torah to the promises given to tortured people at the writing of Revelation, Scriptures cry out for justice, compassion, restoration, and reconciliation.

From the beginnings of Methodism, followers of the Wesleyan movement have maintained an active presence in issues of social concern. Whether it was John Wesley meeting coal miners at the end of their shift or women fighting for temperance in the late 1800s or clergy and laity alike struggling for racial equality in the latter half of the twentieth century, our heritage has been and continues to be permeated with acts of justice.

A few years ago, a youth group created a T-shirt to wear as they became involved in a work camp. The words and images on the back of their shirts say it all: "Revolution—Seek justice, Love mercy, Walk humbly." This reference to Micah 6:8 is indicative of the active faith that characterizes the United Methodist tradition.

During this four-week study, we will explore the various ways that we, through UMCOR, are involved in ministry with the world. We will explore related Scriptures, consider our common heritage as United Methodists, and consider ways we can be in ministry through UMCOR and other avenues of outreach. If you are studying alongside other age groups, using the children's and youth editions of *Being Hope,* you will also have the opportunity to listen and learn from children and youth at the same time you offer your own wisdom. You will discover how we can all work together to be the hands and feet of Christ.

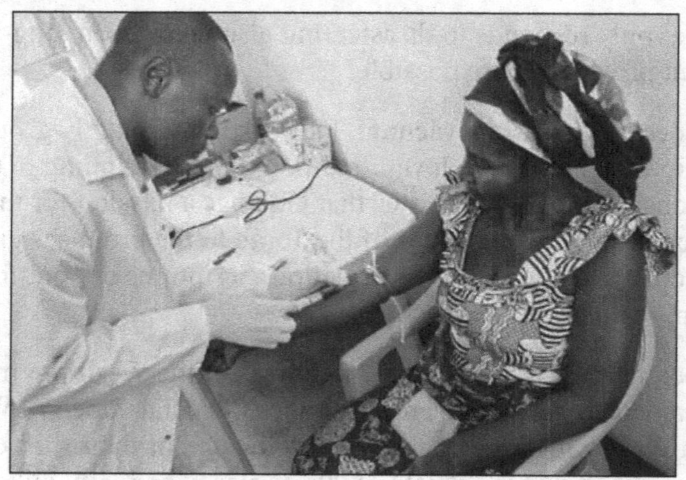

For more information on the work and history of UMCOR, visit *http://www.umcor.org/UMCOR/About-Us.* Annual reports are available for download under the Financials tab of that page.

Session 1

Responding Together: Disaster Response

A legal expert stood up to test Jesus. "Teacher," he said, "what must I do to gain eternal life?"

Jesus replied, "What is written in the Law? How do you interpret it?"

He responded, "You must love the Lord your God with all your heart, with all your being, with all your strength, and with all your mind, and love your neighbor as yourself."

Jesus said to him, "You have answered correctly. Do this and you will live."

But the legal expert wanted to prove that he was right, so he said to Jesus, "And who is my neighbor?"

Jesus replied, "A man went down from Jerusalem to Jericho. He encountered thieves, who stripped him naked, beat him up, and left him near death. Now it just so happened that a priest was also going down the same road. When he saw the injured man, he crossed over to the other side of the road and went on his way. Likewise, a Levite came by that spot, saw the injured man, and crossed over to the other side of the road and went on his way. A Samaritan, who was on a journey, came to where the man was. But when he saw him, he was moved with compassion. The Samaritan went to him and bandaged his wounds, tending them with oil and wine. Then he placed the wounded man on his own donkey, took him to an inn, and took care of him. The next day, he took two full days' worth of wages and gave them to the innkeeper. He said, 'Take care of him, and when I return, I will pay you back for any additional costs.' What do you think? Which one of these three was a neighbor to the man who encountered thieves?"

Then the legal expert said, "The one who demonstrated mercy toward him."

Jesus told him, "Go and do likewise." (Luke 10:25-37)

The disciples decided they would send support to the brothers and sisters in Judea, with everyone contributing to this ministry according to each person's abundance. They sent Barnabas and Saul to take this gift to the elders. (Acts 11:29-30)

After the Explosion

Around dusk on April 17, 2013, an explosion at a fertilizer plant blasted through the community of West, Texas. Fifteen people were killed, 160 wounded, and 150 buildings were destroyed. Like many people when a disaster strikes, the people of First United Methodist Church, Mansfield, Texas, wanted to help. Knowing that well-intentioned people rushing to the site of disasters can often do more harm than good, a group from the church had been trained as an Early Response Team (ERT).

As an ERT, the group was allowed to enter the disaster zone and assist survivors by providing emotional support and stabilizing homes to prevent further damage until the rebuilding phase could begin. "Our training from UMCOR really helped us respond," said Susan Luttrell, the church's director of serving and outreach. "People sat and told their stories, and we were trained and prepared to listen to them."[1]

Theirs was a ministry of presence and healing in the midst of some dreadful situations. It is a ministry that plays out again and again, in different ways, as UMCOR responds to disasters both in the United States and around the world.

---

1. Susan Kim, "After Explosion, Texas Town Stays Strong." 16 July 2013, *http://www.umcor.org /UMCOR/Resources/News-Stories/2013/July/0716-After-Explosion-Texas-Town-Stays-Strong.* Accessed 19 September 2013.

<u>Our Living Past</u>

UMCOR's work is deeply embedded in Scripture. People have responded to tragedy from the earliest times and, according to the Bible, God worked through these people to bring relief. Both of this week's readings focus on men and women responding to the needs of others, although in different ways.

When we read the story of the good Samaritan in the twenty-first century, it loses some of the shock factor that it likely possessed in the first century. For modern readers, the title of the story has become a cliché for people willing to help strangers. Yet, in Jesus' telling, it was a story decrying the boundaries established by good religious people for whom holiness and piety got in the way of doing good. It was the despised (and unclean, by Jewish law) foreigner who was able to provide assistance to the person in need.

This story calls us not only to be willing to stop and help people in random situations or points in our lives, it also calls us to put aside our prejudice and bias and categories in order to be present with people long enough to show them God's love. The Samaritan is also an example of a humble servant who doesn't help the person in need for any reason other than compassion for the other. There is no gain whatsoever for the helper in this story and only the innkeeper knows of his good deed. Finally, the Samaritan provides for the long-term needs of the robbers' victim. Even though the Samaritan can't be present physically, he is "present" long after he leaves the area.

In this Scripture, one person encountered another person in need and reached out to meet that need. The reading from Acts moves in a slightly different direction.

The Book of Acts tells the story of a fledgling church just learning how to fly. Sometimes they got it right; at other times they fell short. One theme remained consistent, however. "An abundance of grace was at work among them all" (Acts 4:33). This abundant grace revealed itself in a consistent ministry of sharing.

In Acts 11, a new congregation was forming in Antioch. An assortment of believers, including Barnabas, spread the news about Jesus. Through their influence, the church gained converts. Paul soon came to their community and stayed for a year. These were the first people to be called "Christian."

Sometime later, a man named Agabus predicted that a famine would engulf the empire. Rather than wringing their hands or storing up supplies, the community of believers chose to support the folks in Judea who were hungry. Scripture says everyone in the Antioch church contributed, "according to each person's abundance" (Acts 11:29).

This passion for reaching out to people in crisis apparently became a mainstay of the larger church in the first century. Paul, on his trips to Jerusalem, brought money to Christians who were impoverished (Romans 15:25-27). In Corinth, collections for the poor were taken on the first day of the week (1 Corinthians 16:2). Macedonian Christians living in extreme poverty gave not only what they could afford but more than they could afford (2 Corinthians 8:2-3).

The Christian imperative to help people in crisis remained alive and well through the centuries. John Wesley is credited as having said, "Do all the good you can. By all the means you can. In all the ways you can. In all the places you can. At all the times you can. To all the people you can. As long as ever you can."

John Wesley lived these words. While still a student at Oxford, he helped found The Holy Club, where a small group dedicated themselves to prayer and study. An outgrowth of their piety soon took shape in the form of reaching out to those in need. It started with prison visits and soon expanded to poor families and the education of children. In later years, Wesley firmly opposed the pollution of water, air, and soil caused by the rapid industrial expansion taking place in England. He started programs to enable women and children to escape the hard life of the mills.[2] Behind Wesley's vehement opposition to the slave trade was his desire to do "all the

---

2. Thomas Kemper, "The Theology of Disaster Relief and Rehabilitation," *New World Outlook*, March–April 2013.

good" he could. One of the major theological contributions of the Methodist movement to Christianity was Wesley's belief that each person could attain both personal piety and social holiness. For Wesley, the two threads of faith were inextricably linked. This dual expression of faith is one of the reasons the Methodist Church has always been involved in social issues.

Beyond Wesley's life, his passion for justice continued to be embodied in the denominations that adhered to Wesley's theology. As early as 1837, The United Brethren Church (one of the forerunners of The United Methodist Church) forbade its members from owning slaves. By the late 1800s, Methodists established schools to help educate former slaves and their children.[3]

But the struggle for justice was never without its challenges. The Methodist Church split twice over the issue of slavery and the role of black members in the early nineteenth century. In the mid-twentieth century, Methodist churches were often rife with disagreement about racial integration of churches and annual conferences. Nonetheless, at the General Conference in 1940, the Methodist Committee on Overseas Relief was instituted, with a goal of providing aid to people overseas who suffered as a result of the Second World War. This "temporary" committee was renewed every four years until 1972, when it became a permanent part of United Methodist ministry.

Preparing Together; Responding Together

Today, the United Methodist Committee on Relief responds to disasters both within the United States and around the world. In 2012 alone, UMCOR dispatched 146,835 volunteers in response to 42 disasters around the United States, 23,544 cleaning buckets for Superstorm Sandy survivors, 32,820 health kits to Hurricane Isaac survivors.[4] Within a month after Superstorm Sandy in 2012, one thousand trained Early Response

---

3. "The Slavery Question and Civil War, 1844-1865," and "Reconstruction, Prosperity, and New Issues, 1866-1913," *The Book of Discipline of The United Methodist Church* (Nashville: The United Methodist Publishing House, 2012); pages 16–18.
4. *The Interpreter,* July/August 2013; page 17.

Team members worked with survivors in Massapequa, New York. These were among more than ten thousand volunteers who have received training over the years.[5] In 2013, UMCOR granted over $1.2 million to seventeen partner organizations and five UMCOR field offices in order to respond to international disasters and provide training to communities in disaster risk reduction. Together, UMCOR, working with its partners, distributed the food, water, clothing, shelter, and provided the training and psychosocial counseling that survivors of disasters in over 56 countries needed this last year. At any given time, UMCOR is engaged in disaster-related activities in more than two dozen countries. Furthermore, UMCOR works wherever it can to provide community-based disaster risk reduction training, helping people find local solutions to local disasters, before they happen.

This work is far more than just putting a Band-Aid on a problem. When UMCOR enters a crisis zone in the United States, it does so with trained volunteer response teams. Long before disaster strikes, UMCOR is busy training Emergency Response Teams (ERTs). These volunteer teams are trained and authorized to work, primarily in their own annual conference, under the coordination of the leadership of that conference. On occasion, annual conferences will make a request for assistance from ERTs located in other conferences. In the face of disaster, UMCOR works with annual conferences, providing technical expertise and emergency grants upon request. Working with local congregations, UMCOR provides essential supplies and emotional support to help people with the immediacy of the disaster.

Part of the reason UMCOR can be on-site so quickly in the United States is that they focus on training local personnel to be effective in disaster recovery management. Trained volunteers working alongside staff members are an invaluable resource wherever communities are affected by storms or other tragedies. UMCOR trains people from local churches, districts, and annual conferences. In addition, they provide guidance in helping church groups and organizations develop disaster response plans so that they will be prepared when emergencies strike.

---

5. Michelle Scott Okabayashi, "'Methodist Angels,' Disaster Response, and You," 31 January 2013. *http://www.umcor.org/UMCOR/Resources/News-Stories/2013/January/0131-Methodist-Angels.* Accessed 19 August 2013.

Within weeks of the tornadoes that roared through Oklahoma in 2013, UMCOR representatives developed long-range recovery goals to help those affected. Their focus was especially directed toward the most vulnerable people who had no insurance and few resources to help them rebuild.[6] UMCOR assistance does not go away when the news grows stale. UMCOR continues to work with annual conferences and churches to help communities rebuild and adapt to their new situations. After a disaster, UMCOR is often one of the last relief agencies to leave.

As in Jesus' story of the wise women who save enough oil for their lamps because they don't know "the day or the hour" of the arrival of the bridegroom (Matthew 25:1-13), UMCOR helps people prepare for disaster. And, like the good Samaritan, UMCOR shows love of God and neighbor by being present, working alongside those who are suffering, providing care even when we can no longer be physically present.

UMCOR utilizes this dual approach of preparedness and response in the U.S. and internationally, albeit with slightly different methodology. In countries outside the U.S., UMCOR provides Community-Based Disaster Risk Reduction Training, working with communities to identify local hazards as well as local solutions. Often, answers to problems are closer than we think.

When staff from UMCOR's office in the Philippines brought relief supplies to the village of Rosaria, following a typhoon in August 2013, they were turned away by villagers, not because they didn't appreciate UMCOR's efforts, but because they were prepared. "We did everything you trained us to do," the village leader told UMCOR staff, "so we are fine. The next village can probably use these materials you brought for us."

Although trained ERTs will occasionally get asked to respond across conference lines in the U.S., non-local volunteers are rarely needed by UMCOR during the disaster response phase in settings outside the U.S. The influx of volunteers into a foreign culture can sometimes become a logistical

---

6. Linda Unger, "Preparing for Recovery in Oklahoma," 7 June 2013. *http://www.umcor.org /UMCOR/Resources/News-Stories/2013/June/0607-Preparing-for-Recovery-in-Oklahoma.* Accessed 19 August 2013.

nightmare for the host organization. Volunteers-In-Mission (VIM) teams are encouraged to make offers of assistance once the disaster response phase has been completed and the affected country is working on rehabilitation. At that point, VIM teams can play an important role in the restoration of church and communities and can provide assistance in many effective ways.

In response to disasters outside the U.S., UMCOR utilizes local partners. UMCOR makes every effort to be good stewards of donated funds. To that end, and to provide specialized resources, UMCOR often works through partner organizations that possess specific skills or in-country knowledge.

Partners are sometimes Methodist entities, sometimes secular non-governmental organizations (NGOs), and sometimes organizations affiliated with other denominations and faiths, in order to gain access to the people in need. UMCOR has found that working with these entities is often the quickest and most efficient way to bring assistance to those in need outside the U.S. context.

When millions of refugees fled Syria to neighboring countries in 2013, UMCOR worked with International Blue Crescent (IBC), to establish a Child-Friendly Space (CFS) in Kilis, Turkey. The CFS is staffed with psychologists and educators that help children deal with the trauma of being forced from their homes in war-torn Syria, as well as providing some remedial educational opportunities. At the CFS, basic nutritional needs as well as the overall well-being of these refugee children are being cared for. Through projects like these, UMCOR attempts to care for children in the way Christ commanded, but also tries to break the cycle of violence by giving children who have experienced the trauma of violent conflict, the possibility of education, play, and a somewhat more "normal" childhood.

UMCOR provides assistance to "the most vulnerable persons affected by crisis or chronic need without regard to their race, religion, gender, or sexual orientation. [As United Methodists,] we believe all people have God-given worth and dignity." This ethic applies not only to how UMCOR works with beneficiaries, but also how it gets the job done. Whenever appropriate in the international setting, UMCOR works within the Methodist connection; but there are also many instances in which the best way, or the only way, to help survivors in certain locations, is by working with agencies outside our denomination. The important work UMCOR is doing in response to the crisis in Syria is a fine example of both the reach and flexibility of UMCOR. "While UMCOR cooperates with other aid organizations to extend our reach, our most important partners are the people we serve. We are confident that successful solutions to emergency or chronic conditions begin with the affected population. UMCOR provides these survivors not only temporary relief but long-term education, training, and support."[7]

When an earthquake devastated Haiti in 2010, UMCOR disaster response teams quickly moved in to provide aid. In fact, UMCOR representatives were already in a Haitian hotel making plans to improve medical services, and two staff members were killed in the building's collapse. UMCOR immediately shifted into high gear, working with partner agencies to provide food, shelter, water, medicine, and emotional support to survivors.[8]

Three years later, UMCOR still made its presence felt. They discovered that some schools did not have clean water. Children were unable to wash their hands before eating and could not even go to the bathroom during the school day. UMCOR helped rectify this situation. They constructed rainwater harvesting mechanisms that provided places for hand washing and clean drinking water. They set up or improved latrines for students and teachers. They also repaired or built classrooms in eleven schools.[9] UMCOR is still present in Haiti and has a five-year strategic plan to empower the communities of Haiti.

---

7. UMCOR Website, "About Us," *http://www.umcor.org/UMCOR/About-Us*. Accessed 5 November 2013.

8. Kathy L. Gilbert, "Haitian Methodists and UMCOR Size Up Needs," *United Methodist News Service,* 24 January 2010, *http://www.umcor.org/UMCOR/Resources/News-Stories/2010/January /Haitian-Methodists-and-UMCOR-Size-Up-Needs*. Accessed 5 November 2013.

9. Jolner Julius, "Water Sanitation and Hygiene for Haitian Children," 5 June 2013. *http://www .umcor.org/UMCOR/Resources/News-Stories/2013/June/0605-Water-Sanitation-and-Hygiene*. Accessed 24 August 2013.

UMCOR is unabashedly Christian and Methodist. In following the way of Christ and the practices of Wesley, UMCOR provides services to people in need, regardless of their religious affiliation, and with no strings attached. For this reason, UMCOR doesn't put tracts or religious messages in its relief kits. These practices allow UMCOR to help people in more countries than some Christian agencies who view relief efforts primarily as a tool to evangelism. Instead, UMCOR views these "acts of mercy" as outward and visible signs of God's love and as a means of grace.

UMCOR's work in disaster response is far more than a nebulous "they" doing something. It is "we" working together. It is churches giving money through One Great Hour of Sharing and through emergency relief offerings. It is people preparing flood buckets ahead of time that can be delivered quickly. It is volunteers spending time at supply depots around the United States preparing relief-supply kits. It is individuals and groups working with Volunteers in Mission to help with rebuilding efforts once the disaster response phase is past. It is United Methodists working together alongside other relief agencies to make a difference.

Whenever disaster happens, the work goes on.

Reflect

- Have you or your congregation been involved in UMCOR's work in disaster response? How? What new information about UMCOR surprised you in these pages?

- What does the story of the good Samaritan say to you about responding to crisis? What does it show you about how best to love one another?

18

- The Antioch church gave to those in need, "according to each person's abundance" (Acts 11:29). Second Corinthians 8:3 reports Macedonian Christians giving "even more than they could afford." How should we decide how much we can afford to give?

- How does your church respond to crises in the world? What efforts have stirred most response or generosity among people in your church? Does your church offer opportunities for discussions about crisis areas and issues of our world? The church can and should be the place we have such conversations with one another.

- What is the message of this chapter for you? How does it inspire you to respond to people in crisis in the future?

Prayer

Lord, we don't always know why disasters happen, but we know you call us to serve those in need, whether near or far. We pray for those who have lost loved ones, homes, belongings, and livelihoods due to tragedy; and we pray for your guidance to put our good will into action. Thank you for all we have, and help us to give generously, knowing that we are just stewards of your good gifts. Amen.

For more information about UMCOR's disaster response work, visit *http://www.umcor.org/UMCOR/programs/disaster-response.*

Session 2

Healing Together: Global Health

Naaman, a general for the king of Aram, was a great man and highly regarded by his master, because through him the Lord had given victory to Aram. This man was a mighty warrior, but he had a skin disease. Now Aramean raiding parties had gone out and captured a young girl from the land of Israel. She served Naaman's wife.

She said to her mistress, "I wish that my master could come before the prophet who lives in Samaria. He would cure him of his skin disease." So Naaman went and told his master what the young girl from the land of Israel had said.

Then Aram's king said, "Go ahead. I will send a letter to Israel's king."
(2 Kings 5:1-5)

Jesus and his disciples sailed to the Gerasenes' land, which is across the lake from Galilee. As soon as Jesus got out of the boat, a certain man met him. The man was from the city and was possessed by demons. For a long time, he had lived among the tombs, naked and homeless. When he saw Jesus, he shrieked and fell down before him. Then he shouted, "What have you to do with me, Jesus, Son of the Most High God? I beg you, don't torture me!" He said this because Jesus had already commanded the unclean spirit to come out of the man. Many times it had taken possession of him, so he would be bound with leg irons and chains and placed under guard. But he would break his restraints, and the demon would force him into the wilderness. (Luke 8:26-29)

Primitive Physick

How would you describe John Wesley to someone unfamiliar with him? Would you say he was a great preacher, or that he was an adept organizer, or that he was a theologian? Perhaps. Would you say he dispensed medical advice? Probably not. Yet that is exactly what he did. Wesley balanced his passion for healing the souls of women and men with an equally strong desire to meet human need. In 1746, the same year that he established a loan program for people in need, he began to reach out to those with medical issues. Physicians and surgeons were around, but only the wealthy could afford their care. The poor were left to fend for themselves. Seeing this, Wesley gathered an assortment of remedies and medicines and began to distribute them at no cost. His efforts were so popular that he soon established a dispensary and, in 1747, published his first volume of *Primitive Physick, or An Easy and Natural Method of Curing Most Diseases*. It was wildly popular and was reprinted in multiple editions during the rest of the century. It was said that John Wesley expected every Methodist preacher to carry a copy of *Primitive Physick* on one side of his saddlebag and a Bible on the other, for the healing of the body and soul.

The medical advice Wesley gave in *Primitive Physick* sometimes seems strange to modern ears, yet much of it is as valuable today as it was then.[10]

His specific advice included the following:

- "The air we breathe is of great consequence to our health."

- "Everyone that would preserve health should be as clean and sweet as possible in their houses, clothes, and furniture."

- "Water is the wholesomest of all drinks; it quickens the appetite and strengthens the digestion most."

- "A due degree of exercise is indispensably necessary to health and long life."

---

10. The preface to Wesley's *Primitive Physick* is available online at *http://www.umcmission .org/Find-Resources/John-Wesley-Sermons/The-Wesleys-and-Their-Times/Primitive-Physick.* Accessed 19 August 2013.

His cures included one for the common cold:

- "Drink a pint of cold water lying down in bed. Or, a spoonful of treacle, in a half pint of water. Or, to one spoonful of oatmeal, and one spoonful of honey, add a piece of butter, the bigness of a nutmeg: pour on gradually near a pint of boiling water: drink it lying down."

Wesley was ahead of his time when it came to hygiene and disease prevention. UMCOR carries on that legacy with a positive approach to health that emphasizes "the leading causes of life," rather than death and despair.

Our Living Past

Two healing stories are featured in the texts for this session, both of them unusual in part because of who was ill.

After Elijah died (or, more correctly, was taken up into heaven), Elisha assumed the mantle of prophecy. Sometime during his lifetime, the king of Aram (ancient Syria) attacked the Northern Kingdom of Israel and prevailed. Naaman was one of the king's generals and presumably participated in the raid. Naaman was considered a great man who boasted many military victories. He also suffered from a terrible skin disease. If his culture was anything like that of the Hebrews, he could and should have been banished from his society.

A slave girl who had been captured in one of the raids worked for Naaman's wife. The slave girl told Naaman's wife about someone in her country who was known as a healer. Through a series of events, Naaman found himself at Elisha's tent flap. Elisha, without even examining the man, told Naaman to wash himself in the Jordan River seven times. The famous warrior did a fair amount of grumbling and resisting. After all, he was a big man in his country. Why should he demean himself to wash in a foreign river? His servants finally convinced him otherwise, he reluctantly did as he was told, and he was cured. Naaman returned to Elisha a whole man and exclaimed, "Now I know for certain that there's no God anywhere on earth except in Israel" (2 Kings 5:15).

One important point of this story is that Naaman was not a Hebrew. He was a Gentile from an enemy nation. Yet Elisha healed him. Years later, Jesus referred to this story when he explained the global nature of his ministry (Luke 4:27).

The New Testament text in some ways parallels the Old. A few paragraphs later in the Gospel, Jesus and the disciples boarded a boat to go to "the other side" of the Sea of Galilee (Luke 8:22). Any time the Gospels say Jesus went to "the other side," it means he entered Gentile country. In this case he wound up in the country of the Gerasenes, which was deep in non-Jewish territory.

While there he came near a cemetery and encountered a man possessed by demons. The man, naked, lived among the tombs. There were all sorts of reasons for Jesus not to associate with the man or the location. For one thing, Jews simply did not venture into Gentile country. It just wasn't done. Then, the tombs themselves were a source of uncleanness. Jews in Jesus' time whitewashed their above-ground graves so that they would not accidentally touch them.

Using your imagination, consider what Jesus' disciples might have been feeling. They were perhaps nervous about being on "the other side" to begin with. Then they approached a cemetery, of all things, and a naked man jumps out at them screaming at the top of his lungs. They must have been wondering if they had better things to do that day.

As abhorrent as the situation was, Jesus stepped right into the messiness of this man's life. He named the demons, transferred them from the man to a huge herd of pigs (also very unclean in Jewish thought), and the man was healed. The owners of the pigs ran to the nearest town, told the news, and brought others out to see what had happened. When everyone arrived, they found the man clothed and very much sane.

Once again, healing took place beyond the borders, on "the other side."

Healing Together

Imagine for a moment that you fly into Kinshasa, the capital of the Democratic Republic of Congo, an equatorial country in Africa that has been ravaged by war during previous decades. Now travel some thirteen hundred miles to the remote community of Kapanga, near the Burundi border. You visit the United Methodist Samuteb Memorial Hospital, a health care facility that serves over 140,000 people. The hospital has a strong childbirth program where an average of two hundred children are born each month. In this remote area, electricity is unreliable, so the staff needs to be creative in finding a way to keep babies warm and healthy. They wrap the baby in a blanket and place the child in a mosquito net-protected cardboard box. Then they place a hot water bottle on each side of the newborn.[11]

The work of Samuteb Memorial Hospital is but one example of the many ways UMCOR is involved in global health programs. There are more than three hundred United Methodist hospitals and clinics worldwide, as well as numerous programs serving vulnerable people in even the most remote communities. UMCOR takes a holistic approach that empowers individuals to adopt healthy habits and develops local resources to sustain improvements in public health long term.

UMCOR's emphasis is on education and prevention as they confront major health issues like maternal and child survival, water and sanitation, HIV/AIDS, and the anti-malaria initiative, "Imagine No Malaria."

---

11. David Tereshchuk, "Strengthening Hospital Care in DR Congo," 20 June 2013. *http://www .umcor.org/UMCOR/Resources/News-Stories/2013/June/0620-Strengthening-Hospital-Care.* Accessed 19 August 2013.

Maternal and Child Survival. Mortality statistics can be staggering. In some countries, 20 percent of children die before their fifth birthday, generally from preventable diseases. It is estimated that every minute, at least one woman dies from complications related to pregnancy or childbirth. UMCOR is among those agencies working to prevent these deaths through such ministries as nutrition programs, training, and immunization. For example, the Nehnwaa Child Survival Project was a recent five-year project. Working with the Ganta United Methodist Hospital in Liberia, this program sought to reduce the death rate of children by 60 percent.[12]

Water and Sanitation. We may take for granted that water drawn from the tap is safe for drinking, bathing, and cooking. For 884 million other people around the globe, this is not the case. In some places water is simply not available; in other locations it is not fit for use. UMCOR's WASH program (Water, Sanitation, and Hygiene) helps communities rehabilitate existing water supplies or dig new wells, and educate the public on prevention of water-borne diseases like diarrhea and cholera that needlessly contribute to the death of millions of children each year. The WASH programs are working to supply the healthiest filtration units to households and train homeowners in their use. The goal is to equip communities to manage their own long-term needs for clean water.

HIV/AIDS. More than 34 million people around the world are affected by HIV/AIDS, the vast majority of them in sub-Saharan Africa. Two-thirds are women, and two million are children. This is more than a disease affecting the poor or those from developing countries, as 1.2 million people in the United States are also infected. The United Methodist Global AIDS Fund aims to diminish these numbers through education, combating stigma in our own churches and communities, prevention, and care programs. Several United Methodist agencies working together support programs globally and locally that focus on prevention, advocacy, testing, and counseling.[13] Congregations and annual conferences are encouraged

---

12. Christie House, "Maternal and Child Survival in Liberia," New World Outlook, March–April 2013.
13. From *http://www.umcor.org/UMCOR/programs/Global-Health/HIV/AIDS/AIDS.*

to participate in the struggle against HIV/AIDS by developing their own programs and participating in World AIDS day on December 1.

Imagine No Malaria. Malaria is a critical health issue in many parts of the world, killing thousands of people each year. Imagine No Malaria partners with other organizations to combat the disease through prevention, treatment, education, and communication. Distribution of insecticide-treated bed nets is an important part of prevention, as is sanitation and the draining of standing water. Diagnostic tools, medicine, infrastructure, and education take prevention efforts even further, with a goal of eradicating this millennia-old disease that has killed millions of people since the time of King Tut.

John Wesley, in *Primitive Physick*, concluded a series of instructions by saying, "To persevere with steadiness in this course, is often more than half the cure." Through the work of UMCOR and other agencies, The United Methodist Church continues to persevere with steadiness toward the goal of empowering communities around the world to resolve their health crises and promote the leading causes of life.

Reflect

- What physicians or specialists have you seen in the last year? What would you do if these resources were unavailable to you for reasons of distance or cost?

- What home remedies have been handed down through your family? Take a look at John Wesley's primitive health-care book. How can your church more fully live out a ministry that cares for the soul and body in your community? In the world?

- What is the message of Naaman's story for you? Do you see yourself in his story, perhaps as the servant girl, Elisha, or Naaman himself?

- What is the challenge to you or your church to go to "the other side"? How should you handle feelings of discomfort that may be involved?

- Of the four areas of global health ministry described here, which touches you most deeply? What might you or your church do to support this or any area of UMCOR's global health program?

Prayer

Lord, we know so many people who are facing crises of health—cancer, infection, heart disease, and more. We pray for their recovery and give thanks for the medical treatment they receive. Make us mindful of those around the world and close to home without access to medical services, or without the means to afford it. Empower us to participate however we can in your work of preventing and treating disease so that all may enjoy healthy, vibrant lives. Thank you that our church is part of your healing work through UMCOR. Show us where our skills, gifts, and resources can be used to give abundant life to all your people. Amen.

To learn more about UMCOR's Global Health programs, visit *http://www .umcor.org/UMCOR/programs/global-health*. For more information on Imagine No Malaria, visit *http://www.imaginenomalaria.org*.

Session 3

Growing Together: Global Development

"The kingdom of heaven is like a landowner who went out early in the morning to hire workers for his vineyard. After he agreed with the workers to pay them a denarion, he sent them into his vineyard.

"Then he went out around nine in the morning and saw others standing around the marketplace doing nothing. He said to them, 'You also go into the vineyard, and I'll pay you whatever is right.' And they went.

"Again around noon and then at three in the afternoon, he did the same thing. Around five in the afternoon he went and found others standing around, and he said to them, 'Why are you just standing around here doing nothing all day long?'

"'Because nobody has hired us,' they replied.

"He responded, 'You also go into the vineyard.'

"When evening came, the owner of the vineyard said to his manager, 'Call the workers and give them their wages, beginning with the last ones hired and moving on finally to the first.' When those who were hired at five in the afternoon came, each one received a denarion. Now when those hired first came, they thought they would receive more. But each of them also received a denarion. When they received it, they grumbled against the landowner, 'These who were hired last worked one hour, and they received the same pay as we did even though we had to work the whole day in the hot sun.'

"But he replied to one of them, 'Friend, I did you no wrong. Didn't I agree to pay you a denarion? Take what belongs to you and go. I want to give to this one who was hired last the same as I give to you. Don't I have the right to do what I want with what belongs to me? Or are you resentful because I'm generous?' So those who are last will be first. And those who are first will be last." (Matthew 20:1-16)

The believers devoted themselves to the apostles' teaching, to the community, to their shared meals, and to their prayers. A sense of awe came over everyone. God performed many wonders and signs through the apostles. All the believers were united and shared everything. They would sell pieces of property and possessions and distribute the proceeds to everyone who needed them. Every day, they met together in the temple and ate in their homes. They shared food with gladness and simplicity. They praised God and demonstrated God's goodness to everyone. The Lord added daily to the community those who were being saved. (Acts 2:42-47)

A New Harvest for Farmers

What tools and resources do you need to do your job? Can you imagine being a carpenter with only a dull saw? Can you imagine being a caterer with only a toy tea set or a sculptor with just some dried-out modeling clay? Imagine being a farmer with old and broken tools, and imagine not having the money or access to rent or buy new ones. This is the dilemma of many skilled, yet struggling, people in countries around the world.

Consider Samvel, who inherited his family's farm in Getap, Armenia. He grew many kinds of fruit trees, but over time his equipment grew outdated and planting and harvesting became more difficult, to the point Samvel considered selling his land and trying to find another way to support himself and his family.

These types of hardships can lead families into poverty, but global development projects can empower individuals and communities to create a more stable, sustainable, and fruitful local economy. In Getap, UMCOR's Sustainable Cooperative Extension and Agricultural Development Program established an agricultural cooperative providing agricultural equipment and technical assistance.[14]

14. Anna Karapetyan, "In Armenia: UMCOR Helps Change Farmers' Lives." 5 July 2013. *http://www.umcor.org/UMCOR/Resources/News-Stories/2013/July/0705-In-Armenia-UMCOR-Helps.* Accessed 19 September 2013.

The parable of the laborers in the vineyard is complicated. It seems unfair by any standard. Why should men who were hired late in the day be paid the same as those who worked from sunrise to sunset? It's just not right!

In Jesus' day, the wealthy found ways to buy up land. Less fortunate landowners were forced off their property, often through foreclosures and insurmountable debt. They lived a hand-to-mouth existence. Since they likely had no artisan skills, they provided cheap labor for the rich farmers, doing the backbreaking work of planting and harvesting. Unemployment was high and there was an oversupply of people looking for work even at menial wages.

In this parable, Jesus talked about leveling the playing field so that generosity replaced normality. In this new economic system, the landowner asked, "Don't I have the right to do what I want with what belongs to me?"

Remember that the landlord in this story is God, not us. This story does not give authority to wealthy landowners, or people who are wealthy relative to most of the world, to do whatever we want with our resources. This story is a reminder that the way God views economics is not the way the world views economics. Whereas the economy of the world runs primarily on an exchange of goods and services, in which labor is traded for money, and the accumulation of wealth often leads to more power and privilege and opportunity, the economy of God is very different.

At the root of the word *economy* is the Greek word *oikonomos,* which has a much less transactional meaning than its English counterpart. *Oikonomos,* more accurately, refers to how a household gets along. In God's economy, then, the household refers to the entire kingdom of God, all people everywhere and all of God's creation. In God's economy, according to Jesus' story of the laborers in the vineyard, there is enough for everyone and everyone has enough. Enough of God's love, but also enough land, water, food, clothing, shelter—the stuff of life.

This desire to have enough to enjoy life on a daily basis is also reflected in Christ's model prayer. Jesus teaches us to pray for "our daily bread," manna sufficient for now, not excessive amounts to be stored in barns, but enough. This is an economics of sustainability for all, not accumulation by a few.

Implementing this kind of economy often runs counter to cultural norms and patterns of consumption in this world. The story of the early church in the Book of Acts begins to illustrate how the *oikonomos* ushered in by Christ might look in practice. Acts 2:42-47 describes the way in which the early church sold possessions and shared resources with one another. For such a description to be mentioned, it must have been a demonstration of extremely uncharacteristic behavior. In the first century Near East, loyalties were first to the extended family, and secondly to those to whom one had debt. These bonds were strong. The early church offered a new economic and social paradigm in which people within the church community had enough and the differences between rich and poor were, albeit imperfectly, narrowed.

This Scripture is all the more challenging for the twenty-first-century reader, faced as we are by the increasingly global phenomenon of consumerism and materialism. With rapid increases in the last fifty years in speed of, and opportunity for, global communication and movement of capital, everyone everywhere can hope for material goods that they never before imagined. This Scripture calls Christians to share with one another even beyond the boundaries of congregation and nation. More than that, this Scripture reminds us that, as the body of Christ, we are to be connected in care with those with needs greater than or different from ours.

It is a question for the ages and a parable that begs us to struggle with it. Do we as individuals, businesses, and nations do what makes sense economically, to benefit those who are already more fortunate, or do we work to create economic stability for all God's people?

Growing Together

UMCOR's work in disaster relief is well known among United Methodists and others. Perhaps it is less well known that UMCOR is heavily involved, not only in ongoing health-related issues, but also in global development. UMCOR seeks ways to provide people with sustainable, self-reliant livelihoods so that they can move out of crisis living into long-term stability.

After the disaster has subsided, many disaster response agencies leave the affected country. Whenever it can, UMCOR attempts to remain behind to work on the long-term development needs of the affected community. Sometimes this is done through continued partnership with local or international organizations as they expand their work in the country. Sometimes UMCOR establishes field offices to further support development work over the long term. It is during this phase that UMCOR and its partners, sometimes including UMVIM teams, come alongside the vulnerable and marginalized to build relationships and communities that are healthy, empowered, and long lasting.

At the core of UMCOR's global development efforts is the concept of sustainability. Sustainability means that the needs of the present are being met without compromising the ability of future generations—children, grandchildren, and beyond—to meet their own needs.

All people of the earth are created in God's image and have creative potential to bring forth fruit and care for creation, to sustain it and watch over and care for it, and to use it in productive ways, not for ourselves alone, but for others. "The earth is the Lord's and everything in it," says Psalm 24:1. But we creatures made in the image of the Creator God are made to creatively watch over, care for, and sustainably use God's creation.[15]

Here are a few ways UMCOR works together in global development for a more sustainable future:

---

15. James, Gulley, "Sustaining and Sustainable Agriculture," unpublished, October 8, 2013.

1. Fair Trade. UMCOR connects United Methodist individuals and congregations with organizations that support fair trade practices. These practices allow workers to earn livable wages and, in so doing, feed their families, provide education for their children, and live more healthy lifestyles. Fair trade organizations include:

- Equal Exchange, a co-op that focuses on coffee, tea, chocolate, bananas, olive oil, and almonds. UMCOR offers Hope's Blend coffee in partnership with Equal Exchange. Designed with local churches' fellowship halls in mind, proceeds from the sale of this coffee help support small-scale farming and quality assurance in Africa (*http://equalexchange.coop*).

- Eco-Palms provides palm fronds for church worship services. These palms are harvested in a way that is both ecologically sustainable and offers fair wages. Eco-Palms also helps provide girls with an education, supports women workers, and creates community centers (*https://www.ecopalms.org*).

- Prosperity Candle works in areas of turmoil and disaster to help women make a living as candlemakers. Ten percent of purchases return to UMCOR to help with other relief programs (*http://www .prosperitycandle.com*).

- SERRV is an international network that helps artisans connect with buyers in a way that provides sustainable incomes to the creators. SERRV stores can be found in some communities in the United States. Local churches can also be networks for selling these products on consignment in their bookstores or at special events (*http://www.serrv.org/category/consignment-umcor*).

2. Hunger and Poverty Grants. UMCOR provides grants to organizations around the world, including the United States, that work to stamp out the root causes of hunger and poverty. To give a few examples among many from 2013, UMCOR helped fund programs that:

- In Armenia, in just one month during 2013, 3,210.80 kg of cheese was distributed, improving the nutritional intake and diet of 7,398 disadvantaged people (2,145 elderly and 5,253 children) living in 7 orphanages, 8 retirement centers, 5 mental and one TB hospital, 5 boarding kindergartens, 28 boarding/special schools, and those who attend 3 soup kitchens and 4 child centers.

- In the first half of 2013, trained 329 participants in five African countries on improved beekeeping, nutrition, and farming techniques.

- Helped 19 communities recover 8,320 square miles of ancestral indigenous territory and begin agriculture, aquaculture, and animal husbandry projects to increase their food security and livelihood potential in southeastern Bolivia, western Paraguay, and northeast and northwest Argentina.

- Trained 40 organizers and agricultural technicians from 24 different Brazilian states on agroecological farming practices, who will then go home and train others, resulting in approximately 700 people trained in sustainable agriculture, resulting in increased food security and environmental sustainability.

- Granted $841,440 to 16 partners working in Liberia, Sierra Leone, South Sudan, China, Moldova, Pakistan, Bolivia, Paraguay, Argentina, Nicaragua, Haiti, Brazil, Palestine, Nepal, India, South Africa, Bulgaria, Brazil, and the United States to carry out programs ranging from water and sanitation and basic education and literacy to livelihood and enterprise development and skills training in nutrition and agriculture.

3. Sustainable Agriculture. UMCOR's primary goal in this area is to
share knowledge. UMCOR trains farmers to care for the earth so that
the earth can care for farmers and their families long into the future.
UMCOR's Sustainable Agriculture and Development program focuses
on ways to promote farming that is relevant to the area and also provides
long-term sustainability (*http://www.umcor.org/UMCOR/Programs
/Global-Development/Sustainable-Agriculture-and-Development/SA-D*).

Sustainable agriculture integrates three main goals: maintain a healthy
environment, produce what we need to sustain life, and ensure that all
people share in the fruit of the earth.

Farmers are people who bring together life-supporting resources to
produce the food we eat. These essential resources of soil, water, and
sunshine provide us plants such as vegetables, grains, and beans, as well as
fish and animals that give us milk and meat, and many, many other things
we like to eat. Farmers have a special role to play in enabling humans
to live and thrive, but all people who touch the soil, use the water, and
enjoy the trees and landscape around us must take care of these valuable
resource gifts. We call that sustainable farming or sustainable agriculture.
But we are all stewards or caretakers of these resource gifts that we did not
create but only received.[16]

Sustainable agriculture—and all of UMCOR's programs—aims to
work together with local resource providers and organizations and local
communities to create solutions that will last long after UMCOR leaves
the scene. In Armenia's Getap Agricultural Cooperative, six months of
startup funds, new equipment, and training helped local farmers learn
new techniques and reinvigorate their business. Starting with twenty-nine
members, the co-op has equipped the farmers of Getap to successfully
take more product to market. Almost four years later, fifty-eight member
farmers utilize the benefits of their locally run agricultural cooperative.

---

16. James Gulley, "Sustaining and Sustainable Agriculture," unpublished, October 8, 2013.

In more than seven African countries, UMCOR is working with a variety of partners to encourage the planting and use of the moringa tree. Tolerant of drought and poor soil, and fast growing, the moringa tree (*M. oleifera*) is a living miracle. Almost every part of the tree, from the roots to the flowers, is beneficial. It can be harvested as food, used as forage for animals, and made into a water purifier, fertilizer, or a variety of traditional medicines. And for the people of many African countries, this miracle tree is a way to combat malnutrition while strengthening food security, sustainable land use, and rural development. This tree, for many communities, has become the tree of life.[17]

Jesus said, "I came so that they could have life—indeed, so that they could live life to the fullest" (John 10:10). UMCOR's global development program works to help people live life to the fullest. This work gives new life in ways that are sustainable. On behalf of United Methodists everywhere, UMCOR works in partnership with the communities we serve to put love into action and share hope for all people.

Reflect

- Where do you get your nutrition? What factors (economic, environmental, physical) would prevent you from acquiring the food you need to survive?

- How do fair trade practices, hunger and poverty grants, and sustainable agriculture programs break the cycle of poverty in at-risk communities?

- Does Jesus' parable seem unreasonable to you? Why, or why not? What do you think is the point of this parable?

---

17. Global Ministries website, "Partnership Works Together to Establish Miracle Tree Forests," April 2012, *http://www.umcmission.org/Learn-About-Us/News-and-Stories/2012/April/Partnership -Establishes-Miracle-Tree-Forests*. Accessed 19 September 2013.

- Are you challenged by the way the early church shared with one another? What would it mean to be that sort of global church in the twenty-first century?

- What strategies do you think do most to alleviate hunger and poverty globally? What about locally? What would be the local equivalent of Fair Trade programs or other strategies that promote long-term self-reliance?

- What new information did you learn about UMCOR's involvement in global development from this session? How could your church get involved in UMCOR's global development work?

Prayer

Lord, give us eyes to see the disparity in our world. Help us to see the human cost of cheap goods and choose to invest in lives and livelihoods so people can earn a fair wage. You have blessed us with so much; bless us also with the humility to take less for ourselves so that others may have enough to live. Amen.

To learn more about UMCOR's global development programs, visit *http://www.umcor.org/UMCOR/Programs/Global-Development.*

Session 4

<u>Serving Together: The Role We Play</u>

I hate, I reject your festivals;

    I don't enjoy your joyous assemblies.

If you bring me your entirely burned offerings and gifts of food—

    I won't be pleased;

I won't even look at your offerings of well-fed animals.

Take away the noise of your songs;

    I won't listen to the melody of your harps.

But let justice roll down like waters,

    and righteousness like an ever-flowing stream. (Amos 5:21-24)

Jesus went to Nazareth, where he had been raised. On the Sabbath he went to the synagogue as he normally did and stood up to read. The synagogue assistant gave him the scroll from the prophet Isaiah. He unrolled the scroll and found the place where it was written:

"The Spirit of the Lord is upon me,

    because the Lord has anointed me.

He has sent me to preach good news to the poor,

> *to proclaim release to the prisoners*

> *and recovery of sight to the blind,*

> *to liberate the oppressed,*

> *and to proclaim the year of the Lord's favor."*

He rolled up the scroll, gave it back to the synagogue assistant, and sat down. Every eye in the synagogue was fixed on him. He began to explain to them, "Today, this scripture has been fulfilled just as you heard it." (Luke 4:16-21)

Neighborology

Rev. Sinnathamby Theavaneson is a United Methodist pastor, born in Sri Lanka, who now lives near Rochester, New York. Not long ago, he preached a sermon based on Jesus' parable of the good Samaritan. In it he said we all know about psychology, anthropology, and theology, but we may not be familiar with a different "-ology": neighborology. Neighborology, he said, is about people. It is about discovering how best we can be neighbors to people no matter who they are or what their status is. It is about being neighbors to the rich and to the poor. It is about being neighbors to the weak as well as to the strong. It is about being neighbors to the uneducated and also to the educated. Even, he joked, it is about being neighbors to both Republicans and Democrats. He said, "Jesus Christ was a neighbor-friendly man. He loved and lived among all types of people. In fact, the name given to him at birth was Emmanuel—God with us."

The day Rev. Theavaneson preached that sermon, a group of twenty-seven youth and adults from that same church arrived in a small community along Lake Ontario to spend a week sleeping at night on the hard floors of a high school and spending their days fixing up homes of folks in that area who needed help. They scraped, they painted, they built decks and wheelchair ramps, and they replaced worn shingles. Most importantly, they developed relationships. The people they worked with were not called homeowners, nor were they called residents. They were called neighbors. The group practiced neighborology.

This final session focuses on neighborology—being in ministry *with* people, not just doing things for them. Later, strategies will be introduced to provide food for thought as you consider how best you or your group or your church can be a neighbor to those beyond your line of sight. Once again, the roots of what you do are embedded in the richness of Scripture.

Our Living Past

Amos was a native of Tekoa, a community in the Southern Kingdom of Judah. He described himself not as a prophet, but as a shepherd and a trimmer of sycamore trees. Yet he ventured into the Northern Kingdom of Israel sometime around 750 B.C. to bring dire warnings of looming disaster if the nation did not return to faithfulness with the one God. In this segment, he was not so much denouncing the religious ceremonies as he was saying that actions needed to correspond with what was said and sung in worship.

In Amos's part of the world, *wadis* are ravines and gullies that are dry most of the year. During the rainy season, however, water flows through them. They carry the potential for sudden and unpredictable flash floods. Amos used the metaphor of a wadi, telling Israel that justice must not occur only occasionally but must be like a continuous stream that flows throughout all the seasons.

Concern for justice is a constant throughout the Bible. It shows up not just in the words of prophets like Amos, but in the Torah laws as well as in the Psalms. It is nowhere more visible than in Jesus' mission statement.

According to Luke, Jesus began his public ministry by teaching in synagogues throughout Galilee. One day he went to his boyhood home in Nazareth. During the synagogue service, the *hazzan* (assistant) handed Jesus the Isaiah scroll. Jesus unrolled the scroll and read in Hebrew the words from Isaiah 61:1. Then he sat down to teach, as was the custom, and announced, "Today, this scripture has been fulfilled just as you heard it." This reading and teaching were the first words of Jesus that are recorded in Luke's Gospel and became the guiding principle of Jesus' ministry.

Jesus had the unique ability to be supremely focused on his relationship with God at the same time that he was tuned in to the needs of those around him. Some have called him a mystic; others have called him a social reformer. In reality, he was both. He lived the words of Deuteronomy by loving God and also loving his neighbors, whoever they were. He invited people to a new world order called the kingdom of God where all God's children had a home, and he worked to bring the Kingdom into reality. He didn't say, "The kingdom is coming." He said, "The kingdom is here, right now."

And so it is. The kingdom of God can be seen wherever people are released from their bindings, whenever the sick and infirm are cared for, whenever the oppressed are liberated, and whenever the jubilee year is proclaimed—a year when freedom is proclaimed "throughout the land to all its inhabitants" (Leviticus 25:10).

Rev. Dr. J. Denise Honeycutt, Deputy General Secretary for UMCOR, points out that we are called to be active participants in that kingdom building. "Mission is from everywhere to everywhere. We are following God into mission—it's God's mission, not ours. All day long God is working for good in the world and God invites us/commands us to be a part of that good work. It's kingdom building work that is led by the Spirit. We, as United Methodists through UMCOR, go in humility to work *with* the most vulnerable and those in great need. We build relationships and learn from one another and are all transformed by the power of God at work within us and among us."

Serving Together

The work of UMCOR is not a nebulous "they" where others do whatever is needed. Instead, UMCOR is a powerful "we" where, working together, change and healing take place. We are the Church of the Poor and those in ministry *with* the poor. Following Jesus' example of servant leadership, those who enjoy greater privileges are called to walk humbly alongside those at society's margins, listening to, learning from, and working in solidarity with them for the transformation of this world. Given that, what follows is a list of ten possibilities for you to get involved with, as an individual, as a small group, or as a church. This is not a comprehensive list by any means, and other opportunities are available at UMCOR's website.

First, however, be warned that there are two things you should *not* do. When disaster strikes, do not send supplies such as clothing to the place where the tragedy took place. It only clogs up the networks of people trying to help and makes things worse instead of better. Second, do not go to the site yourself. Well-meaning volunteers are not needed in the immediate aftermath. This is a time for those who are trained to assess damage and allocate resources. The time for volunteers will come later when networks are set up to coordinate and make best use of those who will come.

Here are ten things you *can* do:

1. One Great Hour of Sharing. One Great Hour of Sharing is a unique, once-a-year offering that provides the foundation stones for UMCOR's work. This offering, usually taken in March, provides the funds necessary for the basics of doing business. UMCOR receives no money from United Methodist World Service or apportionment dollars, which makes One Great Hour of Sharing a vital piece of the puzzle. Money raised here for UMCOR's operating costs makes it possible for **100 percent** of donations made for special causes to go to the designated locations. Operating costs for UMCOR hover around 10 percent. You can find resources and brief videos at *http://www.umcgiving.org.*

2. The Advance. The Advance is The United Methodist Church's way to respond to specific situations. Every dollar given goes directly to the designated cause. When disaster happens, UMCOR will often ask for response funds, and churches will be given a special Advance number with which they can designate their giving. You can also give to general disaster response funds, such as the "International Disaster Response" Advance or the "U.S. Disaster Response" Advance, which permits UMCOR to respond to the many, smaller, unnamed disasters that happen hundreds of times each year. Giving to the Advance is easy to do online at *http://www.umcor .org* and *http://www.umcmission.org.*

3. Relief-Supply Kits. Relief-supply kits help those who are made vulnerable because of disasters, and they also aid people who have no access to basic resources. Collection of supplies for, and assembly of, these kits are great ways to get many people involved in tangible ways, from small children to elderly people who can't easily participate in larger mission projects. Specific instructions on how to make these kits and where to send them can be found at *http://www.umcor.org/UMCOR/Relief-Supplies.*

Relief-supply kits include:

- Bedding kits: sheets, pillows, and pillowcases.

- Birthing Kit: soap, latex or surgical gloves, plastic sheeting, string, razor blades, receiving blankets, plastic bag.

- Cleaning Bucket: five-gallon bucket, liquid laundry detergent, liquid household cleaner, dish soap, air freshener, insect repellent spray, scrub brush, cleaning wipes, sponges, scouring pads, clothespins, clothesline.

- Health Kit: hand towel, washcloth, comb, nail file or clipper, bath soap, toothbrush, adhesive bandages, plastic bag, $1.00.

- Layette Kit: cloth diapers, shirts, washcloths, gowns or sleepers, diaper pins, sweater or jacket, receiving blanket.

- Sewing Kit: Fabric, scissors, needles, thread, buttons, plastic bag.

- School Kit: Scissors, paper, pencil sharpener, ruler, pencils, eraser, crayons, cloth bag.

4. Volunteer. Once an immediate crisis passes and professionals evaluate needs, teams of volunteers are needed to help with cleanup and redevelopment. Additional volunteers are needed to help with long-term rehabilitation projects. You can find out more about specific ways to help by contacting the United Methodist Volunteers in Mission coordinator for your area of the country. Volunteers are also needed at relief supply depots located in Baldwin, Louisiana, and Salt Lake City, Utah, where supplies are collected and assembled so they can be immediately ready when disaster strikes. Contact Sager Brown in Louisiana at *volunteers@ sagerbrown.org* or call 1-800-814-8765. Contact UMCOR West at *westdepot@umcor.org* or call 1-800-973-7250.

5. Early Response Team. Early Response Teams (ERTs) are trained men
and women who move into a disaster site in the days immediately following
a tragedy, offering physical support along with a compassionate presence.
Once trained and certified (and equipped with bright-green T-shirts and
identification badges), their goal is to assist survivors without causing more
harm or being a burden to the community. They might work with children,
install tarps on roofs, or clear out debris, doing whatever is necessary
under the guidance of trained leaders to help with recovery efforts. ERTs
generally work first and foremost in their own annual conferences.

6. Local Church Disaster Plan. With training, local churches can
develop a disaster plan that will enable them to serve their community
when disaster strikes. UMCOR's one-day Connecting Neighbors program
provides churches with the information they will need to develop a plan
that fits their situation.

7. Fair Trade. Individuals, small groups, and churches can participate
in Fair Trade practices and thereby enable small farmers to earn a decent
standard of living. Your church can offer Equal Exchange coffee or sell
fairly traded handicrafts through a SERRV consignment sale.

8. Imagine No Malaria. Get involved with UMCOR's anti-malaria work
by raising money for bed nets, vaccines, and training for health workers.
There is also advocacy work to be done, urging lawmakers to protect funds
for global health. Visit *http://www.imaginenomalaria.org/go-do* for specific
ideas and information about taking action against this preventable disease.

9. Connect, then Collect. There are many ways to get involved in
UMCOR's work around the world. You may be inspired to respond to a
particular crisis or ongoing need by collecting money or supplies. A good
rule of thumb is to "connect before you collect," so that you can contribute
in the most effective way and ensure that your gifts are useful to the people
you want to help. E-mail *umcor@umcor.org* to make a connection that can

guide your church's mission efforts. Connect with UMCOR headquarters before raising funds. Talk with UMCOR's Church Relations Coordinator to learn about current UMCOR projects and activities that might best match your donors' interests. Learn about the area affected by the disaster or where UMCOR is doing the development project (without traveling there) or about the particular development sector or activity.

10. Commit to Pray. Last, but certainly not least, pray for people in crisis, people suffering from disease, disaster, and poverty. Pray for the people on the ground in these places of suffering, working tirelessly to assist vulnerable people and equip communities for long-term stability and prosperity.

Reflect

- What does *neighborology* mean to you? How can you be a good neighbor to people near and far?

- Where do you see the kingdom of God come to life? Do you typically think of God's kingdom as something that will come in the distant future or something here and now?

- Review the list of opportunities. Which of these are the most appealing to you? Select one or more. Work together to develop an action plan. Be specific. Who will be involved? What steps need to be taken? What action can you take in the next twenty-four hours? In a week? In a month? How will you celebrate your success?

- How can you promote One Great Hour of Sharing in your church? What will it mean for UMCOR's operating costs to be covered by this special offering?

- Think back on the Scriptures and areas of mission we've discussed over the past few weeks. What did you discover during these four sessions? What would you still like to learn? What will you do next?

- Now that you have completed this study, go deeper in your understanding of the theology behind UMCOR. Read Global Ministries' "Theology of Mission" at *http://www.umcmission.org/Learn -About-Us/About-Global-Ministries/Theology-of-Mission* and read articles in *New World Outlook*. Study these resources with your mission or other church committee. Prayerfully ask how you can be a part of God's good work in your committee and how can you learn from and be transformed by those you are in ministry with.

Prayer

Lord, let your spirit blow afresh in us, animating our hearts, hands, and feet to serve our neighbors—those close to home and those we will never meet—with your love, in your name. You came to earth to bring good news to the poor, release to the captive, comfort to the sick; and this work goes on through your people down through the ages. Through UMCOR, help us to work together with the poor and those who suffer. We are servants in your kingdom, Lord. Use us as you will. Amen.

COMPASSIONATE

Prayerful

Nourishing

Community

Justice

Supportive

A Partne[r]

PRAYERF[UL]

Strong

Gene[rous]

Justice

Aware